*With love
from*

_____

to

_____

LITTLE☆STARS™

GEMINI

A parent's guide to the little star of the family

JOHN ASTROP

with illustrations by the author

E L E M E N T

Shaftesbury, Dorset ● Rockport, Massachusetts
Brisbane, Queensland

© John Astrop 1994

Published in Great Britain in 1994 by
Element Books Ltd.
Longmead, Shaftesbury, Dorset

Published in the USA in 1994 by
Element, Inc.
42 Broadway, Rockport, MA 01966

Published in Australia in 1994 by
Element Books Ltd.
for Jacaranda Wiley Ltd.
33 Park Road, Milton, Brisbane, 4064

Printed and bound in Great Britain by
BPC Paulton Books Ltd.

British Library Cataloguing in Publication
data available

Library of Congress Cataloguing in publication
data available

ISBN 1-85230-539-8

CONTENTS

THE TWELVE SIGNS 5
LITTLE GEMINI 10
THE BABY 14
THE FIRST THREE YEARS 16
THE KINDERGARTEN 18
SCHOOL AND ONWARDS 19
THE DECANATES 22
OTHER LITTLE GEMINIS 27
THE ARIES PARENT 30
THE TAURUS PARENT 34
THE GEMINI PARENT 38
THE CANCER PARENT 42
THE LEO PARENT 46
THE VIRGO PARENT 50
THE LIBRA PARENT 54
THE SCORPIO PARENT 58
THE SAGITTARIUS PARENT 62
THE CAPRICORN PARENT 66
THE AQUARIUS PARENT 70
THE PISCES PARENT 74
ON THE CUSP 78

THE TWELVE SIGNS

Everyone knows a little about the twelve sun signs. It's the easiest way to approach real astrology without going to the trouble of casting up a chart for the exact time of birth. You won't learn everything about a person with the sun sign but you'll know a lot more than if you just use observation and guesswork. The sun is in roughly the same sign and degree of the zodiac at the same time every year. It's a nice astronomical event that doesn't need calculating. So if you're born between

May 22 and June 21 you'll be pretty sure you're a Gemini; between June 22 and July 23 then you're a Cancer and so on. Many people say how can you divide the human race into twelve sections and are there only twelve different types. Well for a start most people make assessments and judgements on their fellow humans with far smaller groups than that. Rich and poor, educated and non-educated, town girl, country boy, etc. Even with these very simple pigeon holes we can combine to make 'Rich educated town boy' and 'poor non-educated country girl'. We try to get as much information as we can about the others that we make relationships with through life. Astrology as a way of describing and understanding others is unsurpassed. Take the traditional meaning of the twelve signs:

Aries - is self-assertive, brave, energetic and pioneering.

Taurus - is careful, possessive, values material things, is able to build and make things grow.

Gemini - is bright-minded, curious, communicative and versatile.

Cancer - is sensitive, family orientated, protective and caring.

Leo - is creative, dramatic, a leader, showy and generous.

Virgo - is organised, critical, perfectionist and practical.

Libra - is balanced, diplomatic, harmonious, sociable, and likes beautiful things.

Scorpio - is strong-willed, magnetic, powerful, extreme, determined and recuperative.

Sagittarius - is adventurous, philosophical, far-thinking, blunt, truth-seeking.

Capricorn - is cautious, responsible, patient, persistent and ambitious.

Aquarius - is rebellious, unorthodox, humanitarian, idealistic, a fighter of good causes.

Pisces - is sensitive, imaginative, caring, visionary and sacrificing.

If you can find anyone in your circle of friends and acquaintances who isn't described pretty neatly by one of the above it would be surprising. Put the twelve signs into different lives and occupations and you see how it works. A Taurean priest would be more likely to devote his life to looking after the physical and material needs of his church members, feeding the poor, setting up charities. A Virgoan bank robber would plan meticulously and never commit spontaneous crimes. A Leo teacher would make learning an entertainment and a pleasure for her pupils.

So with parents and children. A Capricorn child handles the business of growing up and learning in a very different way to a Libran child. A Scorpio parent manages the family quite differently to an Aquarian. The old boast, 'I'm very fair, I treat all my children the same', may not be the best way to help your little ones at all. Our individual drive is the key to making a success of life. The time when we need the most acceptance of the way we are is in childhood. As a parent it's good to know the ways in which our little ones are like us but we must never forget the ways in which they are different.

LITTLE GEMINI

The moment a little Gemini joins the family it's like switching on an all-electric octopus and forgetting where the on/off switch is. This little bundle of mischief and sheer nervous energy will take you all your time just trying to keep up. It hardly seems that they spend more than a week or two in the helpless baby stage, suddenly they learn to speak, crawl, stand, trot, and gallop everywhere in no time at all. Not for them the long lingering fingering of beloved fluffy toys that gets most cautious babes used to the tough old world. Once little Gemini finds that flopsy bunny doesn't work, doesn't do a

darned thing, 'bun' gets slung in a corner in favour of an experiment with a mislaid can opener, a quick glance at the first two pages of the picture books that Gran brought and what's next? No matter what great ideas you have to keep Junior occupied for more than ten minutes, he'll run through them like an express train. When disappointingly short-lived presents are scattered knee deep throughout the home, you may even see this as a challenge worthy of the trials of Hercules.

OK, maybe this is a little exaggerated but one thing is certain, little Gemini's quest for knowledge gets through a great deal of material in the shortest possible time. Usually precociously bright, they have the ability to be able to do several things at the same time. You'll gasp to find your Geminean student supposedly doing her homework, in her room watching TV with the sound off, listening to

Bon Jovi on a personal stereo, whilst writing an essay on the French Revolution. Just to prove all your indignation wrong, next day she'll get top marks for her essay, be able to discuss the TV programme intelligently whilst humming lightly to herself the more imaginative Bon Jovi guitar solos! Being the first of the Air signs, Geminis are totally on this earth to communicate. Words are important and building a vocabulary the first project once 'Mama' is mastered. The love of talk and discussion will be a prime parent/child interaction in this household. Little Geminis love to pass on their discoveries. In their eternal curiosity and hunger for knowledge they gather snippets of information in a rather trite way. But this all contributes to Gemini's real role as someone who, having understood the many facets of life, can stand back and see the real meaning of the whole.

THE BABY

Like the first sign, Aries, this babe is another kicker, and won't Mom be glad the day little Gemini is born. Wrapped in tight blankets this babe will be free in seconds; those bright little eyes following every new movement in the room should tell you something about this new arrival. After the first few weeks and a crib surrounded by innumerable

rejected soft toys, coloured plastic balls, bells, and fluffy nursery toys you'll realise the low interest factor anything new has for this twitchy little Gemini. It's quite rare for these bright on the move babes to even want a comforting teddy, and security blankets, if needed at all, are frequently changed for other more interesting coloured or textured bits of cloth. This newcomer is not the easiest to predict in terms of regular needs. Smallest Geminis seem to reinvent their schedules every day. Yesterday she cried, hungry at four in the morning; today, bottle ready, you lay awake listening to quiet gurgles of pleasure as she explored the early morning light on the nursery ceiling. Real words will not take long to come and surprisingly early you'll find your new babe imitating your babychat with his own 'scribbletalk' that sounds remarkably like real conversation.

THE FIRST THREE YEARS

Once this little traveller has discovered crawling to be a fairly inefficient means of transport, the swaying totter on two shaky pins is almost immediately followed by the full speed slightly off balance run. Mobile at last!! This is what little Gemini has been waiting for and from dawn to dusk (and sometimes later) they will now be on the move. Trying just to keep your ever-curious Gemini in bed at night time will become a repetitive challenge to your inventiveness. Following you around all day, you'll get question after question, each adding new delicious words to the fast-growing vocabulary. The more you converse with your little Gemini the more fun you'll have. Their minds are bright and perceptive and even in the first two or three years a sharp sense of humour develops where it concerns the clever use of words, so prepare for quite premature snappy back answers that'll have the family in fits of laughter. Although not highly emotional these mentally busy characters are prone to 'moods'.

This may have something to do with the twin symbol for the sign. Suddenly the bright little spark of activity is switched off and replaced with a snappy, morose and almost indifferent little changeling. It may be something to do with recharging the batteries but it happens in Gemini adults too.

You just have to sit this one out; it doesn't last long and when it's over it's as if nothing happened. Early introduction to the social graces will not be wasted at this time. Loving company and making new friends as they do, your little Geminis will welcome you inviting other children to play at home and will surprise you with their confidence in relationships.

THE KINDERGARTEN

No problem taking and leaving behind this little scholar. He won't even notice you go. Running around from group to group and activity to activity, by the end of the first day he'll know everybody, have tried out everything and be organising something new for the next visit. This is probably the best time in childhood for little Gemini: no ties, no schedules, just masses of different things to do (or half do) all day long. Heaven! During this period Junior will develop the best of all Gemini talents, the ability to communicate easily with one's peers.

Although not a leader sign by any means, Geminis always contribute to social gatherings of any kind, quietly keeping things interesting and on the move and even at this early age becoming good arbitrators in their little colleagues' battles.

SCHOOL AND ONWARDS

The business of just accumulating information will be easy for your versatile young prodigy. Allow plenty of time at the end of each school day for the passing on of all the snippets gathered during the school hours. Allow even more for the gossip, who's whose friend and who did what and when. You'll quickly get the idea that school for little Gemini is the most perfectly interesting and stimulating place to be in the world. For the first week that is! Then everything is old hat and the first full flood of enthusiasm fades. Once settled down to the inevitable years of being expected to

do just what everyone else does, the Gemini takes a fairly stable attitude to schoolwork. Fortunately most learning comes easy and with this inventive mind and a 'what she doesn't know she makes up' type of approach there are surprising successes. The great Geminean gift of reading the first couple of pages and making an astute guess at the rest will work all through life so why not get into action as soon as possible. Some school subjects may be a complete turn off, but where the mind can excel then Junior can also. In terms of the other side of school life your Geminean child will feature prominently in all social aspects, undoubtedly popular, never lonely, and always where the action is.

THE THREE DIFFERENT
TYPES OF GEMINI

THE DECANATES

Astrology traditionally divides each of the signs into three equal parts of ten degrees, called the decanates. These give a slightly different quality to the sign depending on whether the child is born in the first, second or third ten days of the thirty-day period when one is in a sign. Each third is ruled by one of the three signs in the same element. Gemini is an Air sign and the three Air signs are Gemini, Libra, and Aquarius. The nature of Air signs is basically communicative so the following three types each has a different way of expressing their mental abilities.

First Decanate - May 22 to May 31

This is the Versatile Communicator. Closest to the true multi-talented Gemini type this one often has several occupations both together and at different times in life. So in childhood it would be surprising to find one of these that didn't show talent playing a musical instrument or two, write quite well, be a pretty good actor, passable chess player and so on. Totally Mercurial they change ideas, locations and friends frequently, experiencing more in one lifetime than half a dozen ordinary mortals.

There is an other world quality about these characters with their sharp-witted intellect and easy ability to sum up any situation on the briefest experience. They just seem to naturally know how things are made, how they work, and how they are operated. Computers and gadgetry of all kinds are no problem for their fastworking intellects, never needing an instruction book to make things work. Good with their hands, and usually uncomfortable if they're unoccupied, they excel in areas where intricate and manipulative work is necessary. Above all they are the communicators supreme, spending hours on the telephone, letter writing and visiting.

Second Decanate - June 1 to June 10

The Harmonious Communicator. Ruled by the planet Venus there is a softening of the brittle Gemini character in this decanate. Less pressured by their own desire for change and movement this part of Gemini puts a greater emphasis on the social aspects of the sign. They love and need the company of others to function fully. Fond of beauty and the good things of life, environments are important. If not artistic themselves, they go to a great deal of effort to surround themselves with artistic friends and activities.

With this decanate there is an ability to help other people understand things which are thought to be too 'avant garde' for most ordinary souls. They can take the seemingly obscure and make it understandable to others. For this reason Geminis from this period make good authors, teachers, presenters in media and, of course, news reporters. In the latter area there are quite a few of these Geminis making injustices public and fighting good causes on behalf of those in society without a voice.

Third Decanate - June 11 to June 21

The Rebel Communicator. The most eccentric and most original Geminis dominate this part of the sign. These are the real rebels that would put their very life at risk for a good cause. Fortunately, with Geminis the best way in which they fight battles is with words and here you will find the sharpest, most astute wit and ability to turn words into swords. Their intellect is such that an idea presented to them will be turned on its head, looked at sideways and shaken mercilessly into something its originator never dreamed of. This, of course, is the stuff of inventors and if you have even the tiniest one, let him or her loose on an old alarm clock and a couple of spent radios and wait and see. This could be the prototype for the gadget that makes the family a fortune. On the other hand you could be harbouring a delightfully entertaining young eccentric. These Geminis care nothing for what others think about them and will pursue their unusual and sideways approached ideas with brilliance all their lives.

OTHER LITTLE GEMINIS

Mums and Dads like you delighted in bringing up the following little communicators. Yours will probably turn out to be even more famous!

First Decanate Gemini

Clint Eastwood, Isadora Duncan, Henry Kissinger, Robert Ludlum, Miles Davis, Joan Collins, Ian Fleming, John Wayne, Laurence Olivier, Charles Aznavour, Wild Bill Hickok, Brooke Shields, Richard Wagner, Queen Victoria, A. Conan Doyle, Franz Mesmer, Bob Hope, Bob Dylan.

Second Decanate Gemini

Marilyn Monroe, Rosalind Russell, Bjorn Borg, Paul Gaugin, Prince, Joan Rivers, Les Paul, Dennis Weaver, Frederick Loewe, Judy Garland, Beau Brummel, Thomas Hardy, Jessica Tandy, Brigham Young, Marquis de Sade, Allen Ginsburg, Cole Porter, Johnny Wiesmuller.

Third Decanate Gemini

Jacques Cousteau, Gene Wilder, Eva Bartok, Lionel Richie, Isabella Rossellini, Jean Paul Sartre, Alice Bailey, Blaise Pascal, George Bush, Chet Atkins, Igor Stravinsky, Paul McCartney, Rasputin, Dean Martin, Steffi Graff, Stan Laurel, Errol Flynn, Jane Russell, Barry Manilow.

AND NOW THE
PARENTS

♈ THE ARIES PARENT

The good news!

You love a challenge and one of the best for you, the Aries parent, could be the Gemini child. Never a dull moment, and if ever the unlimited energy of Aries came in handy, now's the time. Young Geminis from a year and a half onwards are all-talking, all-moving, all-thinking sparkles of restless activity. They take to learning like a duck to water, getting the hang of things quickly and guessing the rest. It's almost better to speak of them in the plural for that's what one of these little wonders feels like. If Aries can deal with all the hows?, whys?, whens? and did you knows? the rest will take care of itself. Aries move into immediate action on any project the moment they think of

it, and so does little Gemini. This should make life easy on both except for one maddening thing. Young Gemini rarely focuses long enough to finish anything; and as it's hardly likely that Aries will accept a 'jack of all trades, master of none' for an offspring, some action will be necessary. You can persuade Junior to stick a bit longer at projects if the reasoning is good, the logic unchallengeable and the prospect stimulating. You'll win if you always explain. Play Gemini's own game for success – keep talking! Aries parents are full of energy and you can be a great help to little Gemini by adding a good proportion of physical exercise, long walks etc., to supplement the mental gymnastics of this little hyperactive. Getting the balance right is a great challenge and it's great to see this youngster, once in a while, falling asleep from physical tiredness rather than sheer mental exhaustion.

...and now the bad news!

If you make your attitude heavy, loaded with reprimands, you'll have a nervy, abstracted little worrier to deal with (oppressed Geminis suffer skin complaints and headaches so watch out for rashes).

Once the attraction of a particular activity has palled little Gemini will pull out of a shared project leaving you feeling foolish. Sometimes this detachment can seem unfeeling and unkind and, if combined with the Geminean love of sarcasm and spiteful words with you on the receiving end, the old Aries blood will rise. Remember that sparkling Geminis can fizzle out like spent fireworks if they overreach themselves and try to keep the challenges light and disposable.

THE TAURUS PARENT

The good news!

You, the calm, steady Taurean parent, could well feel that life with a young Gemini is a perpetual game of Junior Quiztime. Geminis are quick to learn, early talkers and walkers (unless a cautious moon sign slows down the pace), dashing hither and thither picking up snippets of information to feed their insatiable minds. Taureans have a sympathetic understanding of all growing things, and will recognise young Gemini's need for continuous mental stimulation and freedom of movement.

Taurus, however, tackles one job at a time consci-
entiously, and may see Junior's restless diversity
of interests as too scattered to be constructive. For

Gemineans, though,
specialisation is far
too limiting, and a
broad span of knowl-
edge and experience
is more effective in
supporting their own
particular brand of
self-confidence. If
Junior insists that it's
possible to do home-
work whilst watching
TV, with this child you can believe it. Tying this one
down to 'it'll do you good' routines will be like trying to put an octopus in a paper bag. However much
your good sense tells you that reading only the first
few pages of a book and discarding it is a real waste

of hard earned money, try to realise that Junior will have got the gist of what it was all about in the first few pages, be able to talk about it fluently and remember the best bits in six years' time. It's an alien creature you've brought into the world so enjoy and just encourage this versatile and always entertaining one-man band.

...and now the bad news!

You like well-established things, predictable routines, and have the unlimited patience and tenacity to achieve them. Little Gemini has little or no patience, likes the unpredictable and hates rules. If any sign can lose the cool of a calm Taurean it's an irritating, always on the move, fidgety Geminean. Once Dad or Mom dig the heels in and start limiting the freedom, the quicksilver happy little munchkin can turn in seconds into a morose, cold, indifferent, small changeling.

Geminis are not greatly emotional and find it easy to maintain this aloof attitude to their ol' 'stick in the mud' parents for as long as the pressure is maintained. Any household with a Gemini babe has to be prepared for a great deal of scattered and thrown aside unfinished projects, rejected toys, once-played games, half-read books and almost listened to tapes. You'll have a quieter life if you just keep 'em coming, they really aren't being wasted!

THE GEMINI PARENT

The good news!

If anyone could keep up with the physical and mental agility of a little Geminean, it's a big Geminean. You know you're just a big kid yourself anyway! Always carrying the sparkling curiosity of childhood into adult life, Gemini parents find an easy and delightful affinity with this 'like mind'. Gemini households are packed with the 'tools of the trade' that stimulate and fulfil their multifaceted interests. A ready-made hunting ground for Junior. Little Gemini's early mastery of language and movement sets this busy relationship off to a quick start. Usually versatile and talented, these youngsters need enthusiastic help in sustaining interest long enough to achieve tangible results. You'll have to use a bit of Geminean guile to do this, for your own interest wanes pretty quickly too. Changing the venue but keeping to the project can work well for both of you but probably only once. The real value to little Gemini's development will be your constant input of stimulating new material; you like

to keep on the move and this babe will be a pleasure to take along with you. There'll be none of the reluctance of more emotionally based nervous tots; your little sign twin will be two steps ahead of you all the way.

...and now the bad news!

Two problems in an otherwise perfect combination. The first has got to be the almost inevitable fact that you'll tire the living daylights out of each other. Bouncing around like a couple of noisy jumping crackers you'll fizzle out like a damp squib far too often if a slightly less mobile partner isn't on the scene to adjudicate. Then the other thing is the 'moods' – Gemini moods change like the wind and two in the family running the gamut of hot, cold, interested, bored, crazy, serious, may cause a clash or two when they don't coincide. In these duels the weapons are words, often spitefully sarcastic but always quickly forgotten. The mutual need for good companionship is too strong for long-drawn-out battles. The best outlet for any frustrated energies is argument, debate, and discussion. Even the tiniest of tiny Gemini tots can keep a good debate going strong. The rest of the family won't get a word in edgeways.

THE CANCER PARENT

The good news!

For the Gemini child the parent is above all a source of knowledge, information, and company. Your sensitivity will respond quickly to the ever-changing moods of this versatile child. The young Gemini's interests are broad but often short-lived and it can become a full-time job keeping up with the multitude of unfinished activities this child leaves for newer and more absorbing ones. The Cancer parent hopefully will realise that the Gemini child's quest for countless superficial snippets of experience and information are leading to a real understanding of how everything relates to everything else. Little Geminis, one way or another, turn into the communicators of this world. The media, publishing and teaching are full of them, passing on their snippets of information for all the world to share. Now perhaps you'll see the real meaning behind all this seemingly scattered fact gathering. These are not specialists pursuing one field of study for a lifetime, their bright little minds take in fast, just enough information on any subject to understand what's going on. The Cancerian Mom or Dad are great collectors too, although their collections take the form of hundreds of past

memories, family stories and treasured objects. These will be the staff of life to hungry little Gemini and should make for an easy, back and forth, chatty relationship throughout childhood. On the best days (for with both, moods fluctuate) this relationship will sparkle with wit, good humour, and inexhaustible activity.

...and now the bad news!

Conflicts that are likely with this couple will centre around their opposite senses of direction. Nostalgic old Cancer looks back to the way things used to be, and forward-looking Gemini is three jumps ahead. Firmly established Cancerian routines produce snappy answers or sulky withdrawal from Gemini. A different way every day works better when dealing with little Gemini's attention to routine tasks. Cancerians can be softies where their beloved family is concerned, suffering almost anything to keep everyone happy. Your little whizz-kid will soon take in this situation, exploit it to the full, not quite sharing the same depth of feeling for others that you do. It's harder to extricate yourself from this at a later date than setting up firmer ground rules in the first few years.

THE LEO PARENT

The good news!

Proud Leo parents lavish love, affection, and 'no expense spared' comforts on their grateful children. It really is like the indulgent lioness allowing her cubs to romp and play in complete freedom, but ready when necessary to apply a short, sharp cuff of the paw to keep her young ones in line. Leos have a happy knack of dishing out love, affection and a sharp reprimand all in the same breath, so that with little Gemini the point gets taken with no real offence. Young quick-witted Geminis make the transition from cradle and cot to talkative toddler in double quick time. Precocious, amiable and superactive, this busy little companion will enjoy, but never be idle in, your luxurious Leo home. Variety is the spice of Junior's life and, without a little help in maintaining interest long enough to finish a project, attention soon wanders. The helpful Leo may have difficulty in discovering which of

this versatile child's many talents to specifically encourage. All of them, is the answer. The truth is that Geminis are extremely reluctant specialists. Their most successful place in life is where the brilliant all-rounder is essential. Clashes will be few if a good middle line is taken with this youngster: 'You can leave this project if you finish this one' kind of approach.

...and now the bad news!

The biggest danger in this relationship is Leo's encouragement, revelling in the pride of such a talented child, going way over the top and putting much too much pressure on this tiny firecracker. Over-stimulation, just as much as dogmatic restriction, can result in nervous tension (skin rashes and nervous tics are obvious signals for these little hyperactives) or black, black moods. Once resentment sets in, little Gemini's sharp tongue, which can be quite hurtful even in the smallest children, will not suit this regal parent at all. Leos are proud and, no matter how generous, are always the boss. Little whippersnappers just don't talk to the boss like that. A good answer is to let Junior carry on at his own pace and don't push him into the limelight before he's ready, if indeed the limelight is what he wants at all.

THE VIRGO PARENT

The good news!

Keeping up with little Gemini's quick talking, fast moving, dazzle of curiosity and experiment can get most parents puffing with exhaustion. You quick-minded Virgoans, however, are made of sterner stuff. Modestly, and with little fuss, Junior's needs will be met, satisfied and supported by this patient perfectionist. The Virgoan's own well-organised life allows ample time to be devoted to the responsibility of looking after even a whirlwind Gemini. Little Gemini's love of words and incessant chatter will always find quick response, wit, and useful information from this bright-thinking parent. But, and there is a but, Virgo has to finish completely and satisfactorily every job that is tackled. Gemini, on the other hand, can jump from project to project and finish nothing. Strict discipline and calls to duty will only develop this youngster's natural ability for evasion and will achieve little. However superficial it may seem, this scattered energy approach has method when applied to young Gemini's multi-talented, all-round potential. Skilfully managed compromise can get the

necessities dealt with, while leaving this fertile mind free as a bird for all else. Both of you share a love of games and gadgets for quick fingers and faster minds; add a musical instrument or two, calculators, computers, chemistry sets; word games galore; table tennis (must have been invented by a Gemini); encyclopaedias (Gemini reads bits rather than whole books) and nearly always two things at the same time. The message is, provide plenty of stimulation, a well-ordered environment, and little Gemini can blossom and grow to be a credit to your love and care.

...and now the bad news!

You've read it before no doubt, and you know it's more than a little true. You can really be a bit of an old nag when you get going. You're a perfectionist in everything you do and unfortunately in your off moments look for the same perfection in others. There are going to be times when even brilliant little Gemini just won't do anything right, and it'll drive you mad. Not the most thorough of beings, these little bundles of mental energy will leave scattered everywhere unfinished projects, dropped for new ones that look a little more interesting. This unhappily for you and your tidy mind means you'll be spending the next few years in your personal nightmare. A big mess. The more you nag the more little Gemini will sharpen her word power and slanging matches bordering on the downright cruel will become the order of the day. This is a creature of reason, and you'll be surprised how much better will be the response to intelligent sociable discussion rather than straight harsh criticism.

The Libra Parent

The good news!

Little Gemini's inquisitive, nonstop, nervous energy will find an open mind, ready answer, and easy companionship in you, the loving Libra parent. Reason is the Libran strong point, and parental responsibility produces few pompous, dogmatic or authoritarian figures from your sign. Little Gemini will respond well and grow confidently in a tolerant, friendly atmosphere. Keeping up with the speed at which Junior exhausts interest in games, materials, and books can be a Herculean task.

Often happiest doing more than one thing at a time, this 'live wire' can be double the trouble with twice the rewards. Geminis learn fast despite this scattered and seemingly superficial lack of concentration. Their unique view of the world becomes coherent through a natural talent for organising unrelated snippets into a comprehensible whole. The Libran parent's good sense will know how to keep Junior's interest alive long enough to get the basic essentials firmly established. Both of you love words, and discussions will be important from the earliest years, building an easy rational way of dealing with problem situations. This is very often the all too rare relationship where a difficult teenager can still say I can

always talk to Mom or Dad of course. Libran households are usually highly sociable, with much coming and going of friends and other visitors. This will be encouraged in little Gemini, starting early on the business of entertaining her own little visitors and providing good early practice in the art of personal relationships.

...and now the bad news!

The only real snag for this relationship can come from Libra's sometimes exaggerated desire for harmony and peace at all costs. 'Anything to keep the little one happy' will encourage a whirlwind of overindulged whims to the point of spoilt, bad-tempered, nervous exhaustion. Little Geminis, delightful as they can be, have an uncanny knack of knowing your weak points and making the most of this knowledge. Never forget they are sharp as a tack even when the results are to their own detriment. A little Libran balance will save a thousand headaches later. Your ability to see both sides of any situation may have to concentrate on the fact that letting little Gemini have just everything that he thinks he wants may not be good for him. Geminis, like Librans, find most fun in shared activities so share long conversations, storytelling, crafts for adept little fingers, gadget toys and working models, quizzes and puzzles, short trips everywhere.

♏

THE SCORPIO PARENT

The good news!

If any parent can take the nonstop, hustle, bus-
tle and fidgety energy of little Gemini without
batting an eyelid, it's you, Mom or Dad Scorpio.
Proud and devoted parents, the Scorpions root out,
nurture, and boost their little one's talents to full,
confident expression. Ideally, Scorpio's great
strength is in being constantly supportive without
being so obtrusive as to hamper the child's self-
reliance. Rarely finishing any activity before moving
on to the next, young Gemini can exasperate

parents with a more conscientious approach. Scorpio's intuition, however, soon senses the Geminean need for the maximum input of information in the minimum time. The application of a little subtle parental help can convert this potential 'Jack of all trades and master of none' into a positive successful 'all-rounder'. There is sometimes a problem with this relationship in that the light airiness of the Gemini character may sometimes be overawed by the powerful, highly-charged emotional quality of the Scorpio parent. However, normally people of your sign are good natural psychologists, and blessed with this awareness

you should be able to keep the balance just about right. You probably also have the Scorpio's eye for other people's most promising abilities and will know just in what direction to back little Gemini's scattered talents to make the most of them. Scorpios feature strongly as agents and casting directors in showbusiness. It may well be wise, however, to remember that many Geminis succeed in more areas than one and make two careers at the same time. Make sure you don't overlook the fact that versatility is a talent in itself.

...and now the bad news!

You want the very best for your child and with the best of intentions you can sometimes not realise your own strength. If you push little Gemini as hard as you would yourself you may be in for a disaster. Having none of the 'determined attitude that beats a problem at all costs' type of Scorpio mentality, Junior will just seize up if you try to use these powerhouse tactics to get him to do anything. Negatively, the domineering side of the Scorpio nature may result in developing young Gemini's skilful art of evasion. A quick back-answer and swift side step can bring out the worst of this relationship. Scatter the crumbs for your cheeky little sparrow, enjoy the antics and throw the cage in the dustbin. If you get into the habit of doing things together, rather than you directing things from a distance, the relationship should thrive well. You can be an inspiring parent if you don't remain too aloof.

THE SAGITTARIUS PARENT

The good news!

You're open-minded, adventurous and will take parenthood as it comes. The Archer has few fixed ideas, is ready for anything, and has a great interest in understanding little Gemini's needs. Although Sagittarians are not happy to be tied down and may not relish the restriction on their freedom that a small baby causes, there should be less worry on that score with this little bag of tricks. Once little Gemini can walk and talk, which is earlier than most, the real action starts. Memories of the Sagittarian's own inquisitive, adventure-seeking childhood will be awakened by this hyperactive ever-questioning child. No worry now of being restricted for this is the babe that loves being taken everywhere. Small Geminis' love of words turn them quickly into companionable little characters picking up snippets of information and generously sharing it around. These busy quicksilver minds move swiftly from activity to activity just to let you know that variety is the spice of Geminean life.

A little Sagittarian wisdom judiciously applied can extend Junior's staying powers where it matters. An increasing trail of unfinished games, drawings, and discarded projects are, nevertheless, inevita-

ble. Sagittarians have a love of truth that makes them give straight answers to all questions. No beating about the bush for little Gemini, what he wants to know he'll learn from this parent. It might mean that Junior finds out the real story behind Santa Claus and the Easter Bunny a little sooner than most children but that's the nature of this relationship and bright little Gemini had probably worked it out already and was just checking. No big secrets. You get the facts from a Sag!

...and now the bad news!

The 'truth' with an honest Sagittarian can also be the biggest problem. Finding it hard to lie is admirable but dishing out nothing but the blunt truth can be uncomfortable if you are on the receiving end. Little Gemini will be, all too often, and won't like it! If it really hurts, and sometimes it will, Junior will turn your plain unvarnished truth into a vicious slanging match and no one can handle words as weapons like this babe. The other problem is the Sagittarian love of freedom. Should be great for busy little Gemini but, taken to extremes, this easy-going manner can cause problems. 'No limits' can set this youngster aimlessly rushing in every direction at once, burning up energy with no tangible results, and fizzling out in nervous exhaustion. A few well-reasoned guidelines keep Junior happily on the right track.

THE CAPRICORN PARENT

The good news!

Capricorns are calm, patient, and well organised. Little Geminis are hyperactive, impatient, and scatterbrained. At least that's how it could seem to a conscientious Capricornian. They're also sharp as a tack, friendly, precocious and inquisitive. With seemingly little application and no sustained effort, these will-o'-the-wisp youngsters learn with a speed and ease that breaks all the rules in the Goat's book. The temptation to keep the small Gemini concentrating sensibly on one task at a time may often be hard to resist. The need to spread widely (however thin) and take in more experience is a vital part of the versatile Gemini nature. Half-read books, half-finished projects, won't produce a one-track specialist but later Junior's intelligent views on anything and everything will make clear how well it works. Good Capricornian common sense can help maintain interest long enough to finish the necessities. How do you do this? Keep the project alive with plenty of conversation and discussion.

Geminis can always do at least two things at a time and if the chat is interesting enough Junior may not even notice that he's finished his homework for once. What will be appreciated by the Capricornian parent is

the confidence this little whizzkid quickly develops in social situations. Admiring and respecting those that command authority, it will frequently be a delight for you to discover your little scatterbrain talking eloquently to an attentive audience of her seniors. Although both have strong feelings, neither parent nor child are given to great shows of emotion but both need reassurance in different ways. You, the Capricorn, need respect and appreciation for your conscientious application to duty and family, little Gemini needs acknowledgement for his wit and imagination and a good audience to laugh at his jokes.

...and now the bad news!

Your slow but sure approach to life will clash frequently with your offspring's complete lack of application to anything that, to you, seems important. You won't be able to hold back the 'you shoulds', the 'you won'ts' and 'you nevers'. Incessant nagging doesn't do a bit of good and just sends the sparkling energy inwards to produce evasion and twitchy nervous tension (the frustrated Gemini malaise). If you don't want to turn the easy light-hearted Geminean intellect and wit into low cunning then talk to, gently guide, but never rigidly channel this delightful little companion. The more you do together the better. The greatest quality of the Goat is patience and if this is applied in liberal doses to the frequent irritations little Gemini will inflict on you, then the final outcome will repay the effort.

THE AQUARIUS PARENT

The good news!

The stuffy traditional approach to parenthood has no appeal to you. Freedom-loving Aquarians, often avant-garde in the eyes of others with their free exploration of new ideas, make a stimulating bond with inquisitive little Gemineans. These fast-talking, quick-walking infants thrive on just the kind of 'big kid' open interest that typifies the Aquarian. Neither parent nor child is comfortable with clinging displays of affection, but close friendship and mutual respect gives Junior a better basis for security. Keeping up with the way in which little Gemini's quick enthusiasms cool off in favour of the next can be tiring to say the least. The accumulation of scattered playthings and unfinished projects can become an insurmountable problem without help in sustaining interest. Little Gemini's drive is to gain as much diverse information and experience in as short a time as possible. This may seem facile and scatterbrained at first, but it's their way of building early confidence and

understanding of the world as a whole. You care little for what others think, sorting out your own philosophy of life and caring little for other people's opinions of you. You will see this same quality in little Gemini

and be able to enjoy intensely this 'all in the mind' relationship. Barely able to stumble around on two unsteady little legs, your tiny partner will chatter like a sparrow, increasing his vocabulary at breakneck speed as you discuss anything and everything from dawn to dusk. This shared pleasure of just talking to each other will continue throughout life, even getting you moderately comfortably through the emotional teenage years!

...and now the bad news!

Both of you are strong, communicative, freedom loving Air signs, hungry for the new and the unusual. Change is food and drink to you both, and unfortunately if ever there is a problem with this otherwise perfect relationship, this is where it lies. Both thriving on freedom, you can influence each other to extremes of eccentricity. With no limits, little Gemini can over-extend in all directions at once, eventually fizzling out like a spent squib. Nervous twitches are a good warning. Better to limit the menu for this little 'Jack of all trades' and never let her work on more than two projects at a time!

THE PISCES PARENT

The good news!

Warm, loving Piscean parents can be the soft-
est 'touch' in the zodiac. They understand the
shyness and vulnerability of their little charges and
supply oceans of love and reassurance when and
where it's needed. The quick, bright-eyed little
Gemini is rarely shy and less vulnerable than most,
but loves attention. The Piscean need to express
affection may be somewhat hurt to discover this
lovable little sparkle of energy almost immediately wriggles from the warm cuddles to find

something more interesting somewhere else! Little Geminis are not made of the same emotional stuff as the all-feeling Fish, but their needs are equally as demanding. Your great sensitivity should soon sense that what Junior really needs from you is appreciation and a good audience for his sheer

Junior's progress. Bustling with the need for things to do, scarcely starting one thing before looking for the next, 'spoilt' little Geminis can be a nightmare of demands. Soft pedalling the ever-ready Piscean helping hand gives this little one, chance to develop the real Gemini talents. This child's self-reliance, confidence and ease of expression can grow early if imaginatively supported and encouraged. Parent and child share a vivid imagination and sense of fun that should keep the relationship bright and happy.

...and now the bad news!

There is little danger of clashes because you, if you're typical of your sign's qualities, go out of your way to avoid them. Pisceans are notoriously the best at, or the worst for, putting up with unlimited and unbearable situations. However, 'peace at all costs' will bring out the worst of little Gemini's exploitative abilities. If anyone can see an opportunity and make the most of it, it's a quick-witted (and cunning) zodiac Twin. You don't like rows but you should be able to see the need for good healthy argument in little Gemini's make up. Try not to deprive her of this best of all her abilities by always giving in when the backtalk comes thick and fast. Keep arguing, keep it friendly but keep it going. There'll be smiles at the end.

On the Cusp

Many people whose children are born on the day the sun changes signs are not sure whether they come under one sign or another. Some say one is supposed to be a little bit of each but this is rarely true. Adjoining signs are very different to each other so checking up can make everything clear. The opposite table gives the exact Greenwich Mean Time (GMT) when the sun moves into Gemini and when it leaves. Subtract or add the hours indicated below for your nearest big city.

AMSTERDAM	GMT + 01.00	MADRID	GMT + 01.00
ATHENS	GMT + 02.00	MELBOURNE	GMT + 10.00
BOMBAY	GMT + 05.30	MONTREAL	GMT - 05.00
CAIRO	GMT + 02.00	NEW YORK	GMT - 05.00
CALGARY	GMT - 07.00	PARIS	GMT + 01.00
CHICAGO	GMT - 06.00	ROME	GMT + 01.00
DURBAN	GMT + 02.00	S.FRANCISCO	GMT - 08.00
GIBRALTAR	GMT + 01.00	SYDNEY	GMT + 10.00
HOUSTON	GMT - 06.00	TOKYO	GMT + 09.00
LONDON	GMT 00.00	WELLINGTON	GMT + 12.00

DATE	ENTERS GEMINI	GMT	LEAVES GEMINI	GMT
1984	MAY 20	8.58 PM	JUN 21	5.02 AM
1985	MAY 21	2.43 AM	JUN 21	10.44 AM
1986	MAY 21	8.28 AM	JUN 21	4.30 PM
1987	MAY 21	2.10 PM	JUN 21	10.11 PM
1988	MAY 20	7.57 PM	JUN 21	3.57 AM
1989	MAY 21	1.53 AM	JUN 21	9.53 AM
1990	MAY 21	7.37 AM	JUN 21	3.33 PM
1991	MAY 21	1.20 PM	JUN 21	9.19 PM
1992	MAY 20	7.12 PM	JUN 21	3.14 AM
1993	MAY 21	1.01 AM	JUN 21	8.59 AM
1994	MAY 21	6.48 AM	JUN 21	2.48 PM
1995	MAY 21	12.34 PM	JUN 21	8.34 PM
1996	MAY 20	6.23 PM	JUN 21	2.24 AM
1997	MAY 21	12.18 AM	JUN 21	8.20 AM
1998	MAY 21	6.05 AM	JUN 21	2.02 PM
1999	MAY 21	11.53 AM	JUN 21	7.49 PM
2000	MAY 20	5.49 PM	JUN 21	1.48 AM
2001	MAY 20	11.44 PM	JUN 21	7.38 AM
2002	MAY 21	5.30 AM	JUN 21	1.25 PM
2003	MAY 21	11.13 AM	JUN 21	7.11 PM
2004	MAY 20	4.59 PM	JUN 21	12.57 AM

John Astrop is an astrologer and author, has written and illustrated over two hundred books for children, is a little Scorpio married to a little Cancerian artist, has one little Capricorn psychologist, one little Pisces songwriter, one little Virgo traveller and a little Aries rock guitarist. The cats are little Sagittarians.